D1076218

BRIGHT
IDEA
BOOKS

HOW DO ENGINEERS REUSE Rockets?

Arnold Ringstad

raintree

a Capstone company — publishers for children

Raintree is an imprint of Capstone Global Library Limited, a company incorporated in England and Wales having its registered office at 264 Banbury Road, Oxford, OX2 7DY – Registered company number: 6695582

www.raintree.co.uk
myorders@raintree.co.uk

Editor: Megan Gunderson
Designer: Becky Daum
Production Specialist: Colleen McLaren
Originated by Capstone Global Library Limited
Printed and bound in India

ISBN 978 1 4747 7524 3 (hardback)
22 21 20 19 18
10 9 8 7 6 5 4 3 2 1

ISBN 978 1 4747 7348 5 (paperback)
23 22 21 20 19
10 9 8 7 6 5 4 3 2 1

British Library Cataloguing in Publication Data
A full catalogue record for this book is available from the British Library.

Acknowledgements
AP Images: Refugio Ruiz, 23; NASA: 14–15, 28, Bill Ingalls, 13, Blue Origin, 24–25; Newscom: Cover Images, 26–27; Shutterstock: Mykola Mazuryk, cover (background); SpaceX: cover (foreground), 4–5, 6–7, 8–9, 11, 17, 18–19, 20–21, 30–31.
Design Elements: iStockphoto, Red Line Editorial, and Shutterstock Images.

We would like to thank Daniel Kirk, Professor and Associate Dean for Research at the College of Engineering and Computing, Florida Institute of Technology, for his invaluable help in the preparation of this book.

CONTENTS

CHAPTER 1

A THRILLING
Landing

It is a calm day at sea. The sky is blue and the waves are gentle. A wide, flat ship floats and bobs. A huge white X is painted on it.

A special ship moves
into position.

The rocket arrives!

High above the ship, a 120-foot (38-metre) rocket falls to Earth. Wind whips around it. The rocket drops like a stone. Suddenly, a bright flame shoots downwards. A loud cracking sound rips through the air. Metal legs fold out.

The rocket is ready to go back to land. It can be used again later.

The rocket slows. It drops right on the painted X. The flame from its engine stops. The day is calm again.

The ship will carry the rocket back to shore. Then **engineers** will help it launch again.

CHAPTER 2

ROCKETS AT Work

Rockets are vehicles. They travel into space. Some carry **satellites**. Others carry people. All rockets use **propellant**. The engines burn it. Hot gases shoot out of the engines. This moves the rocket forward.

Rockets carry supplies to astronauts in space.

The first rocket went to space in 1957. It launched from the **Soviet Union**. Since then there have been many launches.

Many rockets are used once. They run out of propellant. Then they fall to Earth. They crash into the ocean. New rockets must be built. This takes time and money. Reusable rockets are cheaper. Engineers inspect each rocket after it lands. This makes space travel safer.

In the past,
rockets were
used just once.

13

Atlantis was the last space shuttle used.

Reusable rockets are not a new invention. Space shuttles are one example of them. Space shuttles flew from 1981 to 2011. They had wings and could land like aeroplanes. But they needed many repairs after each trip. They were also very expensive to run. This was a problem. Engineers needed to find a solution.

TONS OF TILES

Each space shuttle had more than 21,000 tiles. The tiles protected the shuttle from heat. Workers had to look at each one before every flight.

CHAPTER 3

THE
Falcon 9

The company SpaceX designs reusable rockets. Elon Musk started SpaceX in 2002. Musk is a businessman. He wants to make space travel cheaper. His goal was to make reusable rockets.

SpaceX rockets have launched from Texas, Florida and California in the United States.

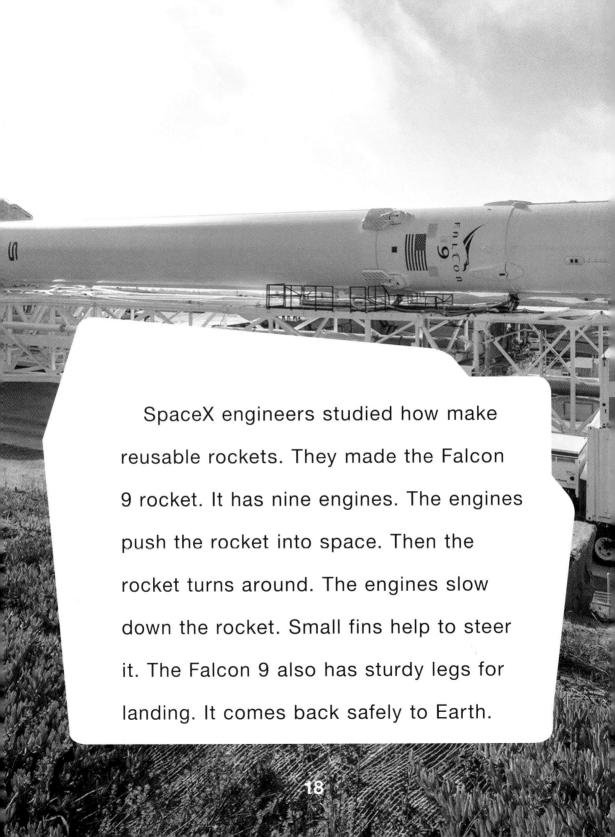

SpaceX engineers studied how make reusable rockets. They made the Falcon 9 rocket. It has nine engines. The engines push the rocket into space. Then the rocket turns around. The engines slow down the rocket. Small fins help to steer it. The Falcon 9 also has sturdy legs for landing. It comes back safely to Earth.

The Falcon 9 weighs 450,000 kilograms (over one million pounds).

SpaceX has also landed rockets safely on land.

STANDING STEADY

A rocket's engines can easily break. Sturdy metal legs support the rocket. The rocket stays steady. This keeps the engines safe. They can be used again.

SpaceX tested the Falcon 9 for years. Some rockets crashed. The company made history in 2015. A Falcon 9 launched from Florida. It delivered satellites into space. Then the rocket turned around. It fired its engines. Its fins steered. Flames shot from its central engine. The rocket slowed down. Its legs unfolded. It landed safely on the ground. Falcon 9 was the first rocket to do this.

CHAPTER 4

ROCKETS OF
the Future

Reusable rockets are the future.
The Falcon 9 is just the beginning. Other
companies are joining SpaceX. They are
making their own reusable rockets.

SPACEX

SpaceX is working on new rockets.

They will be bigger than Falcon 9.

One will have 31 engines. It will carry

100 people into space.

Elon Musk wants to use his rockets to start a city on Mars.

BLUE ORIGIN

Jeff Bezos is another businessman. He is also interested in space. His rocket company is Blue Origin. It made the New Shepard rocket. New Shepard is smaller than Falcon 9. It does not fly as high. It is not as fast. But it is much less expensive.

SAFETY FIRST

Reusable rockets can be dangerous. But New Shepard has a passenger capsule. This capsule has small engines. The engines can get the capsule to safety. They might stop a crash.

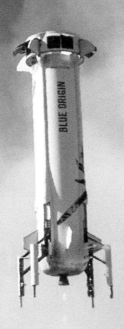

Blue Origin wants many people to travel to space.

VIRGIN GALACTIC

Virgin Galactic is another rocket company. It made SpaceShipTwo. An aircraft carries SpaceShipTwo high in the air. Then SpaceShipTwo lights its rocket engine. It boosts into space. Passengers spend a few minutes there. Then the ship lands like an aeroplane.

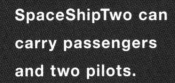

SpaceShipTwo can carry passengers and two pilots.

Engineers are hard at work. They are improving rockets. New rockets will be cheaper. They will carry more people. They may even fly people to Mars!

GLOSSARY

engineer
a person who designs machines or structures

propellant
a material that rockets burn in their engines to push them forward

satellite
a human-made object that is launched into space and travels around Earth

Soviet Union
a former group of countries in Europe, including Russia and the Ukraine

TRIVIA

1. The space shuttle *Discovery* flew more missions than any other shuttle. It went into space 39 times.

2. Elon Musk wants to use reusable rockets for more than space travel. He also wants to use them to fly between places on Earth. A rocket could carry people from New York to China in 40 minutes!

3. SpaceX launched 18 Falcon 9 rockets in 2017. It plans to launch even more each year in the future.

ACTIVITY

SpaceX puts videos of all its launches and landings on YouTube. Ask an adult to help you find one of these videos on the company's YouTube channel. Watch a mission from launch to landing. Then write your own description of everything the rocket does during this time. What things do you recognize from this book? What new things do you notice?

Next, think about how reusable rockets might affect you. Would you want to fly into space on a reusable rocket someday? Why or why not? Write about your opinion.

FIND OUT MORE

Books
Rocketry: Investigate the Science and Technology of Rockets and Ballistics, Carla Mooney (Nomad Press, 2014)

Spaceships and Rockets, Deborah Lock (DK Publishing, 2016)

Websites
Learn more about the reusable rockets made by SpaceX and Blue Origin:
Blue Origin's new Glenn rocket:
https://www.blueorigin.com/new-glenn

SpaceX's failed test :
https://www.youtube.com/watch?v=bvim4rsNHkQ

SpaceX's Falcon 9 rocket:
http://www.spacex.com/falcon9

INDEX